BRYAN ADAMS
THE INSIDE STORY

BRYAN ADAMS
THE INSIDE STORY

HUGH GREGORY

B▦XTREE

First published in the UK in 1992
by Boxtree Limited, 36 Tavistock Street, London WC2E 7PB

Copyright: © Boxtree Limited 1992

ISBN: 1 85283 175 8

Photographs: Retna Pictures Limited

Design: Blackjacks

Printed in Belgium by Proost international Book Production

A catalogue record for this book is available from the British Library.

Contents

7 An Introduction

11 It's Showtime...

15 Early Years

19 The Countdown 1982-84

23 Breakthrough: Reckless

31 Consolidation: Into The Fire

39 Waking Up The Neighbours

46 Discography

An Introduction

A few years ago when Bryan Adams' third album, **Cuts Like A Knife**, was reissued in the UK, a reviewer in one of the popular music weeklies made the following observations about the general attitude towards Bryan's music and others like him: "It's absolutely infuriating that individuals will so often allow their personal reactions and responses to be stifled, their admitted tastes to be governed by the all important rules of cool." This observation seems to me to sum up the case of Bryan Adams: millions like him, and are quite happy to make this admission. There are those, however, who are under the impression that revealing a liking for his music is indicative of some grave character flaw. Which is a pity for them, really.

Bryan Adams isn't the only victim of 'uncool'. There seems to be some sort of overall misconception that, having entered the 1990s, rock 'n' roll is some kind of archaic and arcane style belonging to the dim and distant past. Much of this is due to the fact that rock 'n' roll has become an abstract term that everyone thinks they know the meaning of. They don't. The 'electro-groups' that have dominated the charts in recent years have nothing to do with rock 'n' roll - it's a goodish pose, but not much else. While they all sell records by the truckload, none of them have managed to capture the true spirit of rock 'n' roll.

Bryan Adams is one of the few who has managed to slog his way to the very pinnacle of rock 'n' roll stardom by doing exactly what every 'budding star' is supposed to do in the first place: he goes out and gigs with the regularity of one who has a pack of baying hell-hounds on his trail. It's not a recent attitude, either. His success has been achieved in exactly the same way as The Rolling Stones and The Beatles made their pitches for the Super League: starting right at the bottom in iffy clubs and the like, doing covers of other people's material and learning his trade. That's what rock 'n' roll is all about: taking risks, going out and ripping it up. Many have been very quick to pooh-pooh this very rock 'n' roll stance of his. It is interesting to note how he is slated, more often than not, by the critics for his apparent indifference to the vagaries of the fashion industry: jeans, leather jackets, checked shirts or T-shirts being his standard garb. (Fashion-conscious music journalists have hitherto eluded my notice - they all seem to wear jeans, leather jackets and T-shirts.)

In the final analysis, what has made the difference is Bryan's ability to market, or 'hype', one of his records without appearing to do so; or, as his manager Bruce Allen trenchantly observed, "while some sell a million albums noisily, Bryan sells five million quietly." Everyone understands the concept of marketing or hyping, it is essential in such a saturated marketplace, but it is worth noting that the "allegedly more anarchistic elements" have been the most hyped: The Stones and The Pistols were both putty in

"Look! New shoes!" the hands of marketing men, because of their much-vaunted, and, perhaps, theoretical, anti-social predilections. But then, nobody can blame them for capitalising on the rantings of the gutter press, particularly in the UK, where the tendency for disseminating half-truths is noted the world over. Elvis was hyped more savagely than anybody else: Ed Sullivan wouldn't allow shots on his TV show of the celebrated gyrating pelvis on the grounds that it might corrupt 'minors'. Bryan Adams has managed to steer clear of most of this stuff, not because his reputation is pristine, but because he hasn't actually bothered to become involved in that area of hype where stunts of that nature are obligatory. Throughout he has given the impression of an artist who appears to be impervious to the collective machinations of the media at large. Although, many have scurried around like fury trying to dig up the dirt on this fresh lamb to the slaughter, searching for the Achilles' heel with nagging relentlessness, nothing has emerged.

And so, to these jaundiced ears it seems that Bryan Adams has fulfilled the basic criterion of being a rock 'n' roll star. While his manager Bruce Allen masterminds the development of his career with the acumen of a latter-day Svengali, Bryan has availed himself of the many perks of celebrity but hasn't appeared to compromise himself one iota. Everything he has done has been because he wants to do it. A sweeping statement, perhaps, but close scrutiny of his career to date indicates a guy who is hell-bent on achieving his own aspirations on his own terms.

Evidence of this has been his tireless devotion to his job. He has been prepared to work at it. Very hard indeed. His progress as a songwriter is still maturing. That is the motive force behind his career. His commitment to the ethos and spirit of rock 'n' roll is reminiscent of Keith Richards, Dave Edmunds, Tina Turner, Lowell George (late lamented former member of Little Feat), Bruce Springsteen, John Lennon and probably a few others.

For many of the younger performers emerging, rock 'n' roll still represents a glamorous lifestyle. The image that is still presented on Saturday morning TV is not far removed from the grasping days of Tin-Pan Alley in the 1950s when the music industry was fundamentally manipulative. That aspect still remains, but as long as there are performers like Bryan Adams around and coming through, the ethos and spirit of rock 'n' roll will continue to survive. Hopefully, in each of his audiences there will be one person who will emulate him. And if that is the case, there will still be records in years to come that have the same rawness of ability and energy that he had when he first started off. He has shown that it is possible to crack the big league through native ability and zest. No apparent hype, no funny clothes, in fact none of the supposed concomitants of rock 'n' roll. He just plays his guitar and sings his heart out every time. And that is the object of the exercise.

It's Showtime...

Picture this. An arena or sports stadium, it doesn't matter where it is, what town it's in or what country. It's about eight o'clock in the evening. Hordes of people are streaming towards the venue. They come from all walks of life: some are 'thirtysomething', casually but expensively dressed in leather jackets, cowboy boots and jeans; some are gawky teenagers; but for the most part, they are in their early to mid-twenties. Some of them may be married or just live together in rented accommodation, some of them may still live at home, but the key thing is that almost all of them have loads of disposable income.

This is the face of the average rock 'n' roll audience in the 1990s. At the entrance to the venue, the touts do the rounds gathering up surplus tickets and turning them over to the habitual concert-goer who would never dream of writing off to a booking agency for a ticket, preferring instead to hang around at the entrance to the venue on the off chance that someone will drop a ticket in their direction. Once inside, serried ranks of vendors hawk their wares: burgers, hot dogs, fish & chips, kebabs, beer, coke, Pepsi and, vitally, Official Tour merchandise: baseball hats, T-shirts, badges, sweat-shirts and programmes. Once inside the arena, the gathering crowd find their way to their seats through the slightly acrid, but distinctive, miasma. The PA blasts out a tape on a loop of what the promoter considers to be appropriate music, while the roadies busy themselves on stage, bringing on guitars, fiddling around with amplifiers and generally making their presence felt. The expectant hum of conversation from the audience increases in intensity as the appointed time creeps closer: the houselights dim, the tape from the PA fades and the roadies gradually disappear from the stage. A disembodied voice from the wings announces, "Ladies and Gentlemen, will you please welcome, Brrryyyaaan Adaaams..."

The audience erupts into tumultuous applause, as Bryan Adams runs onto the stage, dressed in T-shirt, jeans and motor-bike boots, followed by his band: guitarist Keith Scott, bassist Dave Taylor, drummer Mickey Curry and organist Tommy Mandel. Not a synth in sight, and as for a drum machine... well as Bryan himself is quick to stress, "If I want to put drums on a record, I want to hear drums, nothing else. And I do find that some of the newer bands don't have the soul of the old records I grew up with - things like AC/DC who have to be one of my favourite bands of the last few years, and John Lennon who sang some of the most classic rock' n' roll ever." This is a no-frills rock 'n' roll show pared right down to basics: no elaborate stage sets, no dry ice (bad for the voice) and no funny costumes.

"How are yer doing out there?," he yells, as he plants his right foot on the stage near the microphone, his left pumping to the beat as he cranks out the opening chords on his guitar and starts to sing. His gravelly voice comes rolling out through the stacked PA, numbering up to 56 speakers.

While the atmosphere is fever pitch from the opening chords, the pervasive aroma of illegal substances becomes more dense. This is the sound of success. Bryan Adams has become one of the biggest draws on the international circuit: from London to Los Angeles, from Paris to Tokyo and from Revelstoke to Auckland, any and every promoter is happy to book him. They know it will sell out in hours, not days. They also know that he won't demand several tonnes of Colombia's finest, nor will he require vast quantities of Jack Daniels to slake his thirst between numbers. For every gig that Bryan plays now, the promoter will receive ten percent of the gross take; the venue will take another ten percent; and Bryan will cover the remaining overheads: the roadies who run the computerised lighting system, tune the guitars and shift the many truckloads of equipment; the drivers; the crew hotel costs; his band and the opening act, when there is one (such is his eminence now that many opening acts would pay him for the opportunity to be the support!). On top of this, Bryan takes a share of the merchandising sales. These are his immediate costs. There are others: fan club and mail order administrators, who work for his manager Bruce Allen; six staff in Allen's office; and, another eight people or so, whose company markets his merchandise. All in all, he employs directly or indirectly about seventy people. It is indicative of the esteem in which he is held by his employees that most of them have been with him for a fair length of time, and many of them would probably be out of work were it not for his endeavours.

In addition to his concert and merchandising revenue, he also earns a substantial income from record sales: in the wake of his recent hit single, **(Everything I Do) I Do It For You**, and the release of a new album, **Waking Up The Neighbours**, after a four year gap, his six albums may well have sold something in the region of twenty million

copies, in total, worldwide by the end of 1991. Additionally, as Bryan has always written his own material in conjunction with Jim Vallance, formerly, and Robert 'Mutt' Lange, latterly, he generates a considerable income from performing rights: every time one of his records is played on the radio or sold anywhere in the world, the respective Performing Rights Society levies a fee of which between 25% and 50% goes to the publisher, while the balance is split between Bryan and his co-writer.

While all of this revenue has been rolling into his company, Adams Communications Inc., of which he is president, he has been largely unaffected by this sudden wealth. His modest lifestyle revolves around a two bedroom cliff-top house in Vancouver with its own recording studio, a collection of fifteen guitars, and that's about it really: he just doesn't seem remotely interested in the traditional trappings of the rock

'n' roll superstar. Despite a penchant for esoteric outdoor pursuits like skydiving and rafting, he is clearly in his element when performing on stage.

His band moves effortlessly through the repertoire: **Kids Wanna Rock** and **It's Only Love**. The audience respond as one voice, all seem to know the words and need little encouragement from Bryan to sing along with him. **Cuts Like A Knife** slices through the air until the audience takes over, with Bryan and the band becoming auxiliaries to the crowd's efforts. Then **Take Me Back** and **Hearts On Fire** follow in swift succession, with the latter engendering another spate of audience participation. It is this that has been the key to his success: he comes across as being so personable that most identify with him. It is a facet of his personality that is evident on stage and in interviews - it never seems contrived.

When he launches into the massively successful hit, **(Everything I Do) I Do It For You**, it is transformed from being an anodyne ballad into an unexpectedly powerful tour de force: the young couples in the audience huddle closer together. Within what seems like seconds, the tempo moves up several notches with **Heaven**, and the crowd as one is on its feet again, punching the air with their fists or flicking lighters or lighting matches. He never allows the momentum to flag for a second: **Can't Stop This Thing We Started**, **Heat Of The Night**, **Hey Honey, I'm Packin' You In**, all punctuated by the odd admonition to the crowd to do whatever. By the time he has launched into the opening bars of **Run To You**, even the most reticent shrinking violet is part of the seething multitude. **Somebody** and **Long Gone** segue seamlessly into one another, providing the conduit to the finale, **Summer Of '69**. The crowd sings itself hoarse and almost takes it over, but as the show reaches its end, the crowd breaks into rapturous applause as Bryan bounds off stage, heading for the dressing room, followed by the members of his band.

But then it's always the same, whenever and wherever he plays, his reception is as tumultuous as it is devoted. However, that reputation and the commensurate rewards have been brought about through sheer effort, hard work and commitment, but it was not always that way, either...

Early Years

Bryan Guy Adams was born on November 5th 1959 in Kingston, Ontario, Canada. He was the first son of an English couple, Jane and Conrad Adams, who had emigrated from Watford to Canada during the mid-1950s. His father, a former major, joined the Canadian diplomatic corps in external affairs; this resulted in the family being almost constantly on the move between countries like Austria, Portugal, England and Israel.

For Bryan and his younger brother Bruce, each change of address meant another change of schooling, usually to establishments set up by the army - both his father and grandfather had spent their formative years at Sandhurst Military Academy in Surrey. Bryan was singularly unimpressed with the strong military traditions in his family and made his contempt perfectly clear to his father. Furthermore, as there was little continuity in his education, he failed to prosper academically and his rebellious nature was constantly getting him into scrapes with the authorities. He was often suspended for infractions and, on one occasion, he was expelled for swearing at the headmaster after kicking a football through his window.

By the time he was ten he had made his intentions clear to his parents about his proposed career in rock 'n' roll by buying an imitation Fender Stratocaster, while on a visit to his uncle in Reading; on the same visit he bought his first album - 'Revolver' by The Beatles. This was to be his first decisive career move and a continuing bone of contention with his father. Despite his tender years he played and practised with the assiduousness of a seasoned professional, often until his fingers bled, much to the chagrin of his father, and listened to records by Creedence Clearwater Revival, John Lennon, The Rolling Stones, T. Rex, Led Zeppelin, AC/DC and Deep Purple. Before long, he had joined his first group: called Shock, they rehearsed at his girlfriend's house until he found her in one of the upstairs bedrooms romping around with some other girl. Unremarkably, the group stopped rehearsing there.

When his parents separated in 1975, he remained with his mother and moved to Vancouver, British Columbia. This change in his circumstances precipitated his next major career move: he left Argyle Secondary School after completing Grade Twelve and spent the $2000 his parents had set aside for the completion of his education at university on a secondhand Estey baby grand piano. With school behind him, he hurled himself into the hurly-burly of the Vancouver music scene, hustling for auditions on one hand and subsidising himself by washing dishes at the Tomahawk Barbecue Restaurant on Vancouver's North Side on the other. One of the first to audition him was Dave Taylor, who was later to become bassist in Bryan's band, but at that time he was looking for a guitarist in his own band. As Bryan only knew three chords at that juncture, he didn't get the job. However, a little later, he joined up with Sweeney Todd, replacing Nick Gilder; the only benefit of this liaison was that it impressed upon him the need to write his own material.

Within the year, he had a stroke of luck that proved critical: he met Jim Vallance at Long & McQuade's music shop on Fourth Avenue, while both were looking at guitars. Vallance was seven years older than Bryan, the drummer in Prism and one of Vancouver's brightest songwriting prospects. He had penned seven of the nine songs for Prism's debut album and great things were expected of the group. Vallance had been looking for a vocalist to perform some of his compositions. Over the next few months or so, they began to develop a song-writing partnership in the basement studio of Vallance's house. This firsthand experi-ence of working within the professional environment of a recording studio gave Bryan sufficient confidence to sign a deal with Irving-Almo of Canada, the Canadian publishing arm of the A&M label. Such was his keenness to be signed that he agreed to the nominal payment of $1. Although it was

a pretty derisory payment, it set him in good stead: at least his material was being published, with Irving-Almo sharing Bryan's publishing rights and revenues. Whether he performed it or it was picked up and recorded by another artist it meant that his name was becoming known and that the company was making money every time one of his songs was played. Quite apart from all this, it provided him with a solid basis upon which to build his career: in years to come, he would renegotiate this contract with better and better terms each time.

The first immediate indication that Bryan had potential as a performer as well as a composer came with the success of his composition, with Vallance, **Let Me Take You Dancing**. It featured Bryan's vocals and went to the top of the disco charts, sell-ing 250,000 copies internationally. His vocals are supposed to resemble Pinky & Perky on a bad day, but the success of the record started a buzz about the new songwriting team, and encouraged A&M Records of Canada to sign Bryan as a solo artist.

It had the further benefit of enabling him to enlist the services of Bruce Allen. Allen was an ex-wrestler, who had grown up

"Get yourself a checked shirt, or you're history!"

in Vancouver during the 1950s. While at school, he had cut quite a dash in a gold lamé suit as the MC at the 'high school hops'. Despite Vancouver's comparative isolation from the mainstream of the music industry in Los Angeles, Allen had gradually established himself as one of the city's prime movers. This had begun to take shape when he started to manage Bachman Turner Overdrive in 1973: between 1973 and 1978 Bachman Turner Overdrive sold around seven million albums. With that success behind him, he started to manage Loverboy, with Lou Blair, and then teamed up with Sam Feldman to form Bruce Allen Talent Promotion Ltd. Now, between the two of them, they have a virtual monopoly of the city's music industry with other businesses like the booking agency S.L. Feldman & Associates, the music publishing company A & F Music and SLF & A Music Services for Film and Television.

Initially, Allen was reluctant to have anything to do with Bryan, but Bryan continued to pester him with demos, showing unwonted tenacity. By December 1979, Allen had conceded and was starting to mastermind Bryan's career, for a fee of 15% of Bryan's gross earnings. He started to pump capital into his protégé's career: at one point, Bryan was indebted to the tune of around $100,000. It was indicative of the mutual trust that, to this day, the only contract between the two was a handshake.

His marketing stratagems couldn't make the first album **Bryan Adams** in 1980 a hit: Bryan's vocals were thin and strained. The songs were rather prosaic and the overall sound lacked bite. However, despite all of these shortcomings, it showed he had promise and that his band, featuring among others, his old friend guitarist Keith Scott, were an almost perfect foil for his rugged brand of rock 'n' roll. Many of the problems with this first album were due to the production, which was handled by Bryan and Jim Vallance: Jim's ability as a co-writer was fine, but he lacked the necessary studio skills

and Bryan, although a quick learner, was too inexperienced. For later albums he enlisted the services of Bob Clearmountain, who was to remain his producer until 1991, when he teamed up with Robert 'Mutt' Lange.

With Allen taking a firm hold of the reins, Bryan started to gig, anywhere and everywhere, appearing at Toronto's El Mocambo, among others. The reality of life on the road - usually in a van weighted with equipment, doing gigs for audiences who only wanted to hear covers of contemporary hits - was brought home with swingeing impact. He took to it like a duck to water. He continued to write with Vallance, working up material for his next album. In order to support himself, he sang on various radio commercials for companies like Thrifty's and Eaton's.

By now, Bryan and Jim were beginning to provide material for other performers. Over the years, a cast of thousands have variously recorded their songs: **Remember** by Bob Welch, **Don't Let Him Know** by Prism, **Lonely Nights** and **Straight From The Heart** by Ian Lloyd - the latter Bryan wrote with Eric Kagna and was to have a hit with it in his own right - **Jump** and **Hometown Hero** by Loverboy, **Another Heartache** by Rod Stewart, **Drive All Night** by Dion, **Edge of a Dream** and **When the Night Comes** by Joe Cocker, **Let Me Down Easy** and **Rebel** by Roger Daltrey, **Nature Of The Beast** by The Law, **Teacher Teacher** by 38 Special, **War Machine** by Instigators, **Back Where You Started** by Tina Turner, **The Best Was Yet To Come** by Laura Branigan, **Can't Wait All Night** by Elkie Brooks, **It Should Have Been Me** by Neil Diamond as well as Carly Simon and, finally, **No Way To Treat A Lady** by Bonnie Tyler and, also, Bonnie Raitt.

Although the superstardom that was to come in later years was still some distance away, he was moving in the right direction and, at least, it was better than washing dirty dishes!

The Countdown 1982-84

When his second album finally emerged in March 1982, entitled **You Want It, You Got It** - although he wanted to call it **Bryan Adams Hasn't Heard Of You Either** - it showed that, not only was his confidence growing as a performer but also his compositional ability was becoming increasingly sophisticated. There was still a slightly pedestrian immaturity but tracks like **Lonely Nights**, **One Good Reason**, **Tonight** and **Don't Look Now** were harbingers of the style that would finally coalesce, and be translated into hard facts with the release of his fourth album, **Reckless,** two years later. Once again, Bryan produced it, but brought in Bob Clearmountain to assist and to mix it. **When You Want It, You Got It** was released in the USA, it climbed to No. 118 and sold 500,000 copies internationally. Two singles, **Lonely Nights** and **One Good Reason** were released, with the former peaking at No. 84 in the USA, thereby giving him his first US hit.

On the back of this success, Allen started to book him onto tours opening for bands like The Kinks, Foreigner and, of course, Loverboy, among others. It represented a slight change in emphasis in his career, because it meant that he was beginning to play larger venues and, therefore, reaching a wider audience. Such was his enthusiasm that he proved to be a hard act to follow for even the most established outfits, but, peculiarly, the bands he was supporting didn't seem to object - indeed many seemed to benefit from having such a sterling opening act. However, it did mark him out as a 'man to mark' to the extent that he was seldom far away from the concert platform and his no-nonsense approach endeared him to those who had never even heard of him before.

While continuing to tour, he carved out enough time in his hectic schedule to go into the studio to record his third album, **Cuts Like A Knife**. As was now customary, it was recorded in under six weeks, with Bob Clearmountain producing. This album came very close to recreating the sound obtained on stage by cutting everything in one or two takes with few overdubs, with tracks like **Straight From The Heart**, **Cuts Like A Knife**, **This Time** and **Take Me Back** already established as integral parts of his live act. In May 1983, he released the single **Straight From The Heart**, which became his first major hit, climbing to No. 10 in the USA. The constant touring was beginning to pay off and when the album was released it reached No. 8 in the USA, becoming his most successful record to date. A tour of Europe was lined up, with his London debut at the Dominion Theatre. While the Dominion was hardly the ideal venue for Bryan's type of music, it brought the music business out in force, only too eager to discover who this guy from Canada was who'd been earning such plaudits from the American press for his live performances. The title track, **Cuts**

Like A Knife, was issued as a single and reached No. 15 in August that year; and in October a third single, **This Time**, ground to a halt at No. 24.

Despite the pressures brought about by touring constantly, he still found the time to cultivate the press, DJs and anybody else who might be remotely helpful. For MTV he was a godsend: here was somebody who personified the spirit of rock 'n' roll and was quite happy to be interviewed, endlessly, if necessary. His natural cockiness charmed all who came across him.

While being adept at the music industry game, he never allowed himself to become

the puppet on a string: the video for the single **Cuts Like A Knife** generated tremendous controversy and airplay into the bargain. It depicted Bryan and his band performing in an empty swimming pool. In the background, a girl stripped behind a screen and appeared in a bathing suit. She dived into the empty pool and came out sopping wet and Bryan was shown holding a flashing knife. Some critics thought it was sexist and in rather poor taste. Bryan's reputed reaction was typically no-nonsense: "Anyone who thinks that it is violent or pornographic is a prude." As far as MTV were concerned, it was just the sort of video

they needed, fusing the twin elements of sex and machismo. By the end of the year he had been on the road for two hundred and eighty-three days.

What with all the touring and his high profile image on video, he got a JUNO Award the following year from the Canadian Academy of Recording Arts and Sciences for the **Cuts Like A Knife** album and a Broadcast Music Inc. Award for **Straight From The Heart** as the most regularly performed song of the year. These tributes to his success confirmed his status as one of the brighter stars in the North American firmament.

Bryan picks up a few chords from old master Dave Edmunds.

Breakthrough: Reckless

His fourth album **Reckless** was released in October 1984. From the time it first emerged it created an impression that was hard to dispel. Many writers and critics were embarrassed by actually liking the record, although few went so far as to admit it, commenting that it was full of cliches and that the sound was due to a multitude of studio gimmicks like exciters on the voice tracks and banks of Linndrums. Unfortunately for the detractors, this wasn't the case. Its success - hitting No. 1 in the USA and spawning six hit singles, including a duet with Tina Turner - was due to the fact that the songs were uniformly well structured and that each had been recorded in one or two takes.

It was mostly recorded at Vancouver's Little Mountain Sound studio and the live feel to much of the record was due to it being recorded principally in the studio's loading bay. Everything was recorded simultaneously, although some of Bryan's guitar parts were overdubbed later on, because he was putting most off his energy into getting the vocal tracks down properly. The whole album took about three months to record and mix, with producer Bob Clearmountain in attendance once again. The simple fact that more time was taken over it cannot fully account for its obvious superiority to its predecessors.

Much of this can be attributed to the improvement in the quality of the songs themselves. This improvement was due, as Bryan himself said to, "becoming more aware of what's essential for you by going out on the road and touring. Being aware of presence and delivering a song – I always believed that the best singers like Paul Rogers and Joe Cocker were those that could make you believe any lyric no matter how boring, or trite it was because of the conviction in their voice." This attitude to songwriting has become a recurrent preoccupation, and consequently his songs "are easy to do live, because they are a band playing in the studio with a real singer and real instrumentation. When people come to see you, they expect to hear the songs live with the same qualities and intensities. You can't do that if they're manufactured." This is why all of his songs are written within a range that is easily reproducible, and although the trademark rasp would appear to be indicative of great strain, Bryan is quick to point out that "you get to know your own limits, and, once you know, you don't exceed them."

Despite the odd track like **Kids Wanna Rock** being rather banal and lyrically just a mite embarrassing, the inspiration was heartfelt. Out of sheer curiosity on one occasion he went to a gig, featuring one of those electro-bands, and "there were all these people in the audience watching this guy on stage fiddling around at a keyboard. Not very interesting, really, and no indication that anybody else was enjoying it all that much."

With the album recorded and bounding up the US charts, he embarked on a world tour that would last thirteen months; this also gave him the opportunity to break in the replacement drummer for Pat Seward of Mikey Curry, adding to the existing line-up of Keith Scott, Tommy Mandel and Dave Taylor. All of whom have remained with him to this day.

On the UK and European legs of the tour, he opened for Tina Turner. This was the vital opening he needed to break through internationally, particularly in the UK, where the album **Reckless** reached No. 7 in March 1985 and the single **Run To You** peaked at No. 11, reaching No. 7 in the USA. It was his first hit in the UK and came closest to defining his sound: the opening arpeggio riff became one of the year's trademark sounds.

Run To You was significant for another reason apart from registering his first hit in the UK: while shooting the video in London with director David Mallett, he met Vicky Russell, daughter of film director Ken Russell, who had been enlisted on the shoot as costume designer. It was the beginning of a relationship that lasted for over six years. For the next month, the two of them flitted from one side of the world to the other with the ease of professional social butterflies. Friends and acquaintances dubbed them "The Twins", as they launched into a series of serious spending sprees, courtesy of all the major credit card companies. While both were boisterous and noisy, with a tendency on occasions to hurl food around in the swankiest of restaurants, neither was in the least overwhelmed by the other.

For Bryan, here was a girl who was totally undaunted by the rigours of touring and was completely indifferent to the degree of his success. Furthermore, she egged him on, encouraging him in any crazy stunt he might get up to next, which was all a bit of a departure for him as he had always tended to give the impression of being quite shy. Cocky, sure, but never one to indulge in the

Bryan and Vicky Russell. "There's a bluebottle up there, Vicky ..."

"It's mine!" "No, mine!" "No, mine!" "I saw it first!"

traditional high jinks of the rock 'n' roll fraternity.

Vicky, on the other hand, had grown up in the spotlight of her father's often controversial career. Throughout her adolescence, she was usually on location: USA for *Crimes Of Passion*, Spain for *Valentino*, Central Europe for *Mahler* and *Lisztomania* and England for *Tommy*, *The Boy Friend* and *Savage Messiah*. In most of these films, she made cameo appearances: most notably as 'Sally Simpson' in *Tommy*. Consequently, she'd been surrounded by film stars like Oliver Reed, Robert Powell, Glenda Jackson, Michael Caine, Helen Mirren and Twiggy all her life and so, rubbing shoulders with famous rock 'n' roll stars was no big deal.

Her background in the film business had given her little or no interest in the mechanics of the music business: reputedly, while working on a video for former Eagle Don Henley, part of her brief was to make the guitarist resemble Keith Richards - she had

no idea who he was! Furthermore, the filming of *Tommy* left her with few illusions about the glamour of the music business as the role of 'Sally Simpson' represents the negative side of rock 'n' roll and, although Vicky was only twelve at the time, it made an indelible impression upon her. This impression was reinforced by the confrontations she had with the odd fan here and there, who convinced her that it was potentially dangerous to be taken in by the alleged glamour of the music industry. Similarly, she was totally unfazed by life on the road, as there was little difference from being on location. A case of same meat, different gravy, the only difference being the fans.

While Bryan and Vicky began to spend more and more time together, his career moved into overdrive. The tour was proving to be a runaway success with the **Reckless** album beginning to sell well in Europe as well. Some of this was due to opening for Tina Turner, whose own popularity was beginning to reach its height, but the well-oiled stage show that he had now perfected left few doubts in the minds of those who saw him that superstardom was just around the next corner.

Needless to say, Bryan's close proximity to Tina caused any amount of speculation in the press that while performing in Hawaii they had started to have an affair. It was, of course, rubbish, causing great hilarity for Vicky and Tina, who were both completely impervious to the machinations of the press. But for Bryan it was a bit of an eye-opener as he had never been subjected to this type of speculation about his private life before and as far as he was concerned he had never been in the slightest bit interested in getting involved in the usual rock 'n' roll star bit - he just wanted to play. The plus side of all this speculation was the fuelling of sales of both

Bryan shares the stage with Tina Turner's legs.

the album and the steady trickle of singles from the album: **Somebody** in April, which went to No. 11 in the USA and No. 35 in the UK; **Heaven** in June, which had the distinction of being his first US No. 1, despite only reaching the comparatively lowly No. 38 in the UK.

On July 13, he appeared on the bill at Live Aid at JFK Stadium in Philadelphia with a host of luminaries like Bob Dylan, Mick Jagger, Daryl Hall & John Oates and Tina Turner. Quite apart from performing, Bryan was also to compose the Canadian contribution to the USA For Africa LP, **We Are The World**. The composition **Tears Are Not Enough** was written with co-writer Jim Vallance and Chicago's erstwhile producer David Foster. Among the other Canadian artists featured under the collective name of Northern Lights, were Neil

For the Prince's Trust concert, Bryan joined in the attempt to break the Live Aid stage packing record.

Young, Joni Mitchell, Richard Manuel of The Band, Burton Cummings formerly of Guess Who, Dan Reno of Loverboy, Corey Hart, Gordon Lightfoot, Dan Hill, Anne Murray, Carole Baker, Ronnie Hawkins, Geddy Lee of Rush and John Candy.

With the success of this appearance at Live Aid, where he was rubbing shoulders with the rock 'n' roll aristocracy, and combined with his own shows, he was suddenly catapulted into the ranks of those who could fill stadiums in seconds. Another single from the album **Reckless**, entitled **Summer Of '69**, was released; it had all the anthem-like qualities guaranteed to set concert audiences reverberating in years to come. This wasn't properly reflected in charting terms as it only reached No. 5 in the USA and No. 42 in the UK, but then most had got the album anyway by this time. Similarly, the next single, **One Night Love Affair**, only got to No. 13 in the USA, and failed to make any impression on the UK charts whatsoever. The sixth and final single from the album was saved for the Christmas period.

This was **It's Only Love**, the duet with Tina Turner. With his customary adroitness, Bryan's manager Bruce Allen had managed to ensure that his charge would be guaranteed maximum exposure at the most critical time of the year. It was a very nifty piece of manoeuvring on both Allen's part and Rodger Davies', Tina Turner's manager: the latter was only too happy to allow Bryan's record company A & M to foot the bill for the video and all of the other promotional ploys. Speculation was still rife about the alleged affair

At Live Aid in Philadelphia there were almost as many people on stage as there were in the crowd.

between Bryan and Tina; and the sight of the two of them performing together on the video for the single fired up album sales for both of them no end, with each benefitting from the attention of the other's audience. The single reached No. 15 in the USA and No. 29 in the UK.

The main thing, though, was that by recording with Tina, he had acquired the veneer of respectability, becoming, almost, a bona fide member of the rock 'n' roll aristocracy. He was no longer the middle range rock 'n' roller with delusions of grandeur, he had properly arrived in the upper echelons and had become accessible to a slightly older age group at the same time. This was borne out by the sales of **Reckless**, which has sold in the region of ten million copies worldwide and is still in the UK album charts, having re-entered on the back of the success of the single **(Everything I Do) I Do It For You**. In addition to the phenomenal sales of **Reckless**, it also gave him a clutch of JUNO Awards from the Canadian Academy of Recording Arts and Sciences: **Reckless** was named Best Album, Bryan was named Best Male Vocalist and Bryan and Jim Vallance were named the Best Songwriting Partnership. All of these accolades established him as the best-known face in Canada, leaving national figures like Pierre Trudeau, Wayne Gretzky and Brian Mulroney shrouded in comparative anonymity. Following hot on the heels of the duet, he set the seal upon his status as a major league performer by issuing the seasonal single, **Christmas Time**; it only reached No. 55 in the UK. But then, nobody releases Christmas singles until they have really arrived!

Despite the pervasive aura of celebrity that has threatened to engulf him he has continued to appear to be the personification of the guy next door who just wants to have a good time, irrespective of risk.

There is a story of how, in Memphis in June 1985, while touring, Bryan and some of the other members of the crew decided to go parachuting on their day off. Bryan jumped with a trained parachutist, but the main chute got tangled around their legs and wrapped around their faces. The trained parachutist panicked so Bryan was left struggling to save both their lives and make the auxiliary chute function. The fact that it did was fortuitous, but the fact that Bryan appeared totally unfazed by the whole episode, saying something to the effect of "Let's have a beer" when they landed, illustrates a coolness of temperament that belies his comparatively tender years.

The scrapes of his school years still remained, with occasional prankish outbursts that fully justified Tina's nickname for him of 'Dennis the Menace'. In these, he was ably abetted by Vicky, who showed herself to be an ever-willing accomplice on his japes, but when it came to performing and doing his job he was the model of professionalism.

Consolidation: Into The Fire

Throughout 1986, he worked on the material with Jim for the follow-up, his fifth album, to **Reckless**, doing the odd concert here and there. In the meantime, his reputation in the UK was fuelled by a brace of reissues - **This Time** and **Straight From The Heart**; neither had made a significant impression first time around, but in the wake of a little controversy sparked by the English press and the reissue of his third album **Cuts Like A Knife**, the former reached No. 41 and the latter No. 51.

The controversy came about as a result of Bryan performing the composition **Diana** at a soundcheck for a concert that he was headlining to mark the visit of the Prince and Princess Of Wales to Vancouver's Expo '86. The English paparazzi, trailing the royal couple and desperate as ever for any titbit of gossip, immediately latched upon the lyrics of the song, claiming that it was directed at the Princess Of Wales. The tabloid press had a field day with headlines that must have made all immediately concerned fall around in helpless laughter: priceless epithets like "STAR'S LOVE SONG TO DI IS BANNED ...... BUT CHARLES CAN'T STOP HER FLIRTING"; "FACE TO FACE: THE PRINCESS AND THE DOTING ROCK STAR ...... " and "AXED! ...... SONG FOR DI". Throughout the furore Bryan kept a low-profile, allowing the machinations of the press to run riot.

When the hoop-la died down, Bryan took to the road once again with U2, Peter Gabriel and Sting for the Conspiracy of Hope Tour on behalf of Amnesty International to draw attention to the plight of political prisoners the world over. His involvement in the Conspiracy of Hope Tour prompted some to accuse him of jumping onto the political bandwagon. But as he was to say himself later on: "I suppose I did it mainly for myself. It was an organisation that I wanted to learn more about, and that was the best way to do it. Young people in Vancouver don't appear to know much about it, and perhaps my involvement would encourage them to find out more. I think that maybe it was the best tour I've ever done, because every night was inspired, and I was never stuck for anything to do."

As the momentum of the tour picked up, so the size of the venues increased. By the time the tour was nearing its conclusion, they were performing at eighty thousand-seaters and there was the potential to sell out these venues several times over. While the cumulative effect of his participation was to heighten his profile, it did make many aware that some of his material was just as lyrically sensitive as Sting's or Peter Gabriel's, and that he wasn't just another bozo lining his pockets.

Just before the release of **Into The Fire**, Bryan appeared at one of the Prince's Trust Charity Concerts in London, in the presence of the Prince and Princess of Wales. The press were out in force to try and ascertain whether there was any truth in the

Bryan displays one of his massive range of checked shirts.

At the Amnesty International Press Conference, Bryan wore dark glasses so that everyone would know he was a rock star.

rumours about Bryan being besotted with the Princess of Wales. They couldn't. All they could dredge up was that the Prince of Wales had said that Bryan's music made his sternum vibrate.

Into The Fire was finally released in May 1987. The practical side of recording the album had differed from that of its predecessors in that it was recorded in his own home. While the success of this approach was conclusive in the reduction of recording costs, which would have been prohibitive within a traditional studio set up, it had also afforded him the luxury of extra time enabling him to experiment. Each instrument had been recorded in a different part of the house: the drums in the dining-room, the organ in the bathroom, the bass in a clothes closet and the guitars and vocals in the living-room.

At the Amnesty International Concert, the fans were so overwhelmed that they spontaneously transmuted into pot plants.

Furthermore, he had been able to spend a lot more time working on the material with Jim Vallance: between November 1985 and August 1986, the two of them wrote for up to twelve hours a day, six days a week. As a result, the lyrical content of the album had undergone a sea change. Up until that point, the lyrics had solely addressed the problems of growing up: being in love, loneliness, insecurity and haplessness. But here there were songs like **Native Son** - referring to the demise of the North American Indians - and **Remembrance Day** - dedicated to a relative of Vallance's who had died in the First World War. For Bryan, like Vallance, had "come from a real family of military people too. My father was very pro-military - and still is - and my grandfather. The best days of his life were during the war. Not necessarily the war itself - just the times, because

there was a great camaraderie then that people never forget. There isn't that kind of union of males working together now. The unions are getting abolished. Look at the coal miners' situation, where all they've done all of their lives is to work in the mines and now with the way technology is developing, they lose their jobs. And, perhaps, that camaraderie is what war's all about, that sort of male, macho flexing of muscles."

There were other indications of his willingness to make a stand over issues that concerned him. In the first instance, he was invited by the makers of the film *Top Gun* to contribute **Only The Strong Survive** to the soundtrack. Despite a very lucrative offer, he declined on the grounds that he disliked the way the film attempted to glamorise war. Secondly, in 1986 a fleet of US navy nuclear warships were anchored in

Vancouver's harbour. Bryan wrote to the newspaper, Vancouver
Province, complaining of the fleet's presence as Vancouver was
ostensibly a 'nuclear free zone', and their presence violated that
status. Needless to say, this letter prompted a heated exchange
among the city elders, who found his views somewhat unpalatable.
While **Reckless** had pushed him into the big time league of major
artists, **Into The Fire** and his appearances at major charity gigs
established him as a voice that could appeal not just to the romantic
inclinations of the young rabble-rousing concert-goer, but also to an
older, more socially aware audience.

In addition, it made critics start to take him slightly more seri-
ously and criticise him more strenuously, as the general perception
hitherto had been that of another Bruce Springsteen imitator. Most

of the criticisms were just a part of the routine bad-mouthing that is always a feature of any performer's career when a change of direction appears or massive success has been achieved.

In Bryan's case, he had made the cardinal error of releasing an album that showed that he had got a brain in his head and was aware of world issues and was quite prepared to make his feelings known. Never a popular move. Furthermore, having aligned himself with certain members of the rock 'n' roll aristocracy on the Amnesty International Tour, he was immediately targeted by some sections of the press as being another of 'these bleeding hearts'. Other critics said that the album lacked the impact of its predecessor, with one claiming to have counted fifty-odd rock 'n' roll clichés. The fact that much of it had been written prior to the Amnesty tour eluded most.

Bryan and Ian Gillan try out new and innovative headphone positions.

Bryan recruits a new band member - somebody called Elton John.

Despite its failure to generate the same volume of sales that its predecessor had done, **Into The Fire** climbed to No. 7 in the USA and No. 10 in the UK. As per usual, a fistful of singles were released. The first was **Heat Of The Night**, which reached No. 54 in the UK and No. 6 in the USA. It was followed by **Hearts On Fire**, which petered out at No. 26 in the USA and No. 57 in the UK, and **Victim Of Love**, which climbed to No. 32 in the USA and No. 68 in the UK.

In the wake of its release, Bryan set off on the traditional world tour. This tour lasted nine months and underlined the financial growth in his status as a performer, yielding some $45 million in ticket sales and $15 million in merchandising - badges, T-shirts, sweat-shirts and programmes. At Christmas 1987 another seasonal offering, **Run Rudolph Run**, appeared; it had been recorded on June 3rd at the Marquee Club in London and was included on the Special Olympics Charity album, **A Very Seasonal Christmas**, reaching No. 20 in the USA and No. 40 in the UK.

As the tour neared its completion he appeared at the Freedomfest at Wembley Stadium in London, honouring Nelson Mandela's seventieth birthday. It was another indication that he was nearing the pinnacle of superstardom, just by the invitation to appear at what was a politically sensitive event and the acknowledgement that he was potentially sympathetic to the Anti-Apartheid cause. Over seventy thousand people turned up to see a bill that boasted U2, Peter Gabriel, Sting and Terence Trent D'Arby, as well as Bryan.

With the tour completed, he returned to Vancouver to start working on new material for the next album. For the next three years or so very little would be heard of him apart from the odd gig here and there: the difference now was that 'the odd gig' usually involved an audience of anything up to 100,000 people.

Waking Up The Neighbours

At the end of the **Into The Fire** tour in early 1988, he took time out before embarking on the next album. He had been on the road almost constantly for the past seven years. In that time his reputation had flourished and he had had little opportunity to savour the extent of his success. There were other things that had cropped up in the interim, not least of which was the thorny problem of finding a new songwriting partner to replace Jim Vallance. He, too, had begun to find a new level of success, as a result of his involvement with Bryan.

The break-up of the partnership had not been specifically acrimonious, but it had caused a certain amount of tension. As a result of his success with Bryan's earlier albums, Jim had been wooed by other bands like Aerosmith, who were so impressed by his work with Bryan that they wanted him to work with them. Bryan, not unreasonably, was pretty reluctant to continue working with somebody who couldn't offer a full-time commitment and who, clearly, had his own busy schedule. While Bob Clearmountain was fine as an engineer and studio technician, one of the best in the business, he was certainly no co-writer. Another co-writer was necessary. The right person didn't emerge immediately, however.

Throughout the remainder of 1988, and most of 1989, Bryan worked at preparing material for his next album, punctuated by occasional visits to various studios to guest as guitarist or backing vocalist on records by Motley Crue, Dion, Joe Cocker and Belinda Carlisle, among others. Despite the less gruelling schedule than usual, he still flitted around the globe, often with Vicky, with extraordinary regularity. In April 1989, he appeared in Moscow for the satellite telecast of the World Music Video Awards to an estimated audience of over seven hundred and fifty million viewers worldwide. In between, however, he managed to spend more time at his home, pottering around the cliff-top garden, tending the roses, and following up a keen interest in the paintings and writings of Emily Carr.

In December 1989, A & M issued his first live album – entitled **Live Live Live**, it was only released in Japan. It went gold immediately. After the release of the live album, he rounded off 1989 with two shows on New Year's Eve at the seventy thousand-seat Tokyo Dome. In the meantime, he had been working on material for the new album: Steve Lillywhite had been brought in as producer. Steve had produced everyone, including The Rolling Stones, Simple Minds, Peter Gabriel, Psychedelic Furs, Joan Armatrading, Big Country, Kirsty MacColl and U2, and was widely regarded as being one of the better rock 'n' roll producers. By the time nine tracks had been laid down, Bryan decided that they just weren't what he was aiming at. A case, perhaps of still not having found what he was looking for. It was at this juncture that Robert 'Mutt' Lange was enlisted.

Mutt had come to prominence by producing and co-writing Def Leppard's formidably successful albums, **High 'n' Dry** (1981), **Pyromania** (1983) and **Hysteria** (1987), all of which had collectively sold well over twenty million copies worldwide. Def Leppard had been a pretty average rock outfit from Sheffield, until Mutt had lent a hand with the material. They were transformed overnight, selling albums by the truckload, particularly in the USA, where they became ranked alongside Aerosmith, Bon Jovi, Grateful Dead and other titans of rock as one of the biggest audience draws in the country.

Bryan started to record in London at Battery Studios, having moved from The Warehouse in Vancouver. Mutt began the long and laborious process of rebuilding the existing material. All of the material was subjected to his intense and meticulous scrutiny: taking it to pieces, restructuring, reshaping and re-recording simultaneously. This represented a completely different approach to recording to Bryan's earlier methods with Jim Vallance and Bob Clearmountain, when the material had been recorded substantially as it had been composed. Having laid down a track, Bryan was able to jet off and do other things, leaving Mutt and Bob Clearmountain, who had been retained to mix the tracks, free to work on the track, knocking it into shape.

On June 30, he kept up his unflagging itinerary with an appearance before an audience of seventy-five thousand at a festival in Mitfyns in Denmark. This was followed by another festival appearance before an audience of eighty thousand at Roskilde, also in Denmark. On July 21, Bryan appeared at the performance of **The Wall** at Potzdamer Platz in Berlin.

The Wall, written by Roger Waters, formerly of Pink Floyd, was being staged to raise funds for various disaster relief operations, on the site of the recently demolished Berlin Wall. While it was for charity, it was also a highly personal gesture on the part of

Waters, whose father had been killed at the Battle of Anzio in 1944. The whole project had come about as a result of a meeting between Waters and the founder of the charity, Group Captain Leonard Cheshire VC.

In September 1989, Cheshire had instigated a Memorial Fund to cope with all the natural disasters like Hurricane Gilbert and the earthquake in Armenia as well as "unnatural" disasters like Chernobyl. The target for the fund was five hundred million pounds: in other words, five pounds for each person killed in war this century. When Waters and Cheshire met, they got on immediately and the site of the recently dismantled Berlin Wall was the ideal venue to stage a show for charity.

In comparison with the considerable scale of the undertaking, assembling a cast for the spectacle was relatively simple. Apart from Bryan, who performed **Young Lust** and **What Shall We Do Now?**, other artists involved included Sinead O'Connor,

Van Morrison, The Scorpions, Rick Danko and Levon Helm of The Band, Cyndi Lauper and Joni Mitchell; other celebrities like Albert Finney, Marianne Faithful, Jerry Hall, Tim Curry, Ute Lemper and Thomas Dolby were also on hand to lend added credence to the theatrics. In the end, the spectacle drew a huge audience of some two hundred and fifty thousand, with an estimated television audience of around one billion.

Bryan's presence tended to underline his own highly personal attitude and commitment to making stands on behalf of causes with which he was sympathetic. His participation in **The Wall** was, perhaps, predictable given his own family's military background and the intensity of his disagreements with his father over military matters. As was also predictable, Bryan's contribution was one of the less histrionic. No mean achievement, in itself, for such an emotionally charged occasion.

Doctor Adams examines Natalie Cole's tongue at the Mandela benefit concert at Wembley ...

With **The Wall** out of the way, Bryan returned to London to continue work on the album with Mutt and Bob, which he would continue to do for the next twelve months or so. Shortly before his appearance in Berlin, he became the first recipient of the Order Of British Columbia: the order had been instituted under legislation passed a year earlier to honour those who had made a significant contribution to the province.

By June 1991, the album was effectively finished with only bits of remixing to be completed. Bryan took to the road with ZZ Top, playing the European festival circuit. Among the venues they played were the Mungersdorf Stadium in Cologne and Milton Keynes in Britain: other artists on the bills included Little Angels, John Farnham, Thunder and The Law. While ZZ Top were the undoubted headliners with elaborate stage sets, it was Bryan who, even playing second fiddle, stole one show after another. The cruise around Europe was followed in August by what was almost a local concert at Revelstoke in British Columbia, sponsored by the Canadian provincial government, the object of the exercise being to take rock 'n' roll out of the big city arenas and into the rural backwaters. Although the concert and others similar featuring artists like Linda

Ronstadt and Hammer were very successful in themselves, the sponsorship of some twenty-six million dollars to encourage tourism in British Columbia and neighbouring Alberta seemed a mite excessive for a public relations exercise.

However, these were the first steps in oiling the cogs of the promotional wheels for the release of the sixth and most difficult album, **Waking Up The Neighbours**. It had been three years in the making and had eventually cost three times its projected budget. As a foretaste of the album, a ballad entitled **(Everything I Do) I Do It For You** was released. The basic melody had

been passed on to Bryan by Michael Kamen, who was scoring the film, *Robin Hood: Prince Of Thieves*, starring Kevin Costner. The film's producers had tried to get a variety of artists such as Julia Fordham and Sinead O'Connor, to perform the song. Nobody had been that interested. Bryan went to work on the song with Mutt, writing the lyrics and restructuring the melody, adding the middle eight and rearranging the break. The lyrics were perhaps the easiest part as Bryan had split up with his longtime girlfriend Vicky not long before. Not that it was intended as a tribute to her, more that he was in the right frame of mind for writing

a ballad. When the song was passed on to the producers, rumour has it they were not unduly impressed. This theory is vindicated by it being used over the closing credits of the film. It went straight to No. 1 in the USA; in the UK, it went to No. 1 where it remained for sixteen weeks, the longest period of time a record had stayed at No. 1 in the UK. Previously, that honour had belonged to Slim Whitman, whose **Rose Marie** had occupied the top spot for eleven consecutive weeks in 1955. By the end of its run, it had been No. 1 in thirteen countries.

When the album was eventually released in September 1991, it went straight into the charts on both sides of the Atlantic in the top ten - in the US at No. 6, and in the UK at No. 1. Throughout, the distinctive hand of Mutt was at work, lending added muscle to Bryan's vocals. Despite the length of time it had taken, the wait was worth while, showing his total commitment to his music and his intention to make each and

every track stand on its own account. Bryan had often mentioned in past interviews the frequency with which albums were crammed with duff material, not offering any sort of value for money to fans. With this album, he tried to ensure that no such charge could be levied against him.

Before release it had generated two hit singles, the second being **Can't Stop This Thing We Started**, which hit No. 7 in the UK while its predecessor, **(Everything I Do) I Do It For You**, was still at No. 1. Lyrically, **Can't Stop This Thing We Started** seemed to provide a metaphor of sorts for Bryan's own career. Other tracks like **Is Your Mama Gonna Miss Ya?**, **Hey Honey, I'm Packing You In**, **All I Want Is You** and **Thought I'd Died And Gone To Heaven** all seemed - in very different ways – to bare all the hallmarks of hit singles. Even **Don't Drop That Bomb On Me**, which harked back to the seriousness of the **Into The Fire** album, was notable for its

immediacy despite the rather preachy connotations of the title.

Quite apart from the all-round appeal of the album, there were certain sectors who disapproved of his new writing partner, Mutt Lange. The Canadian Radio-Television and Telecommunications Commission, the federal broadcast regulator, decided that all fifteen songs on the new album were "un-Canadian". What that statement meant in practical terms was that there were restrictions on the number of times his songs could be played on FM radio stations. The fact that, as a Canadian, he had collaborated with an English writer, was the cause of the problem, although they carefully ignored the fact that there were no restrictions on non-Canadian artists who were in the charts at that time, like Rod Stewart and Bonnie Raitt. It all seemed a rather pointless gesture as it was aimed at the songwriters, those who require the greatest support and tend to be the hardest to find.

In late October, he headed for the UK and Ireland, playing a series of concerts in Belfast, Dublin, Aberdeen, Glasgow, Whitley Bay, Sheffield, Birmingham and London. All sold out in seconds, confirming his status as one of the biggest concert draws around. The London dates were distinguished by the appearance of Slim Whitman for a duet on **Rose Marie**; while very much Whitman's song, Bryan's single verse seemed to bring a lot more resonance to what is a pretty trite song. For the rest, the shows were models of expertise, with the new material bearing the well-worn imprimatur that years of use generally entail.

The press on the UK tour seemed to hold the view that the greatest threat to his popularity lay in his intrinsic "ordinariness" and no-nonsense approach, and that this was in danger of becoming a cliché in itself. But, then, it was only the critics that seemed to take that line. Everybody else, including Bryan, just had fun!

DISCOGRAPHY

SECTION 1: THE ALBUMS

BRYAN ADAMS
(A & M Records)
producer Bob Clearmountain
UK release date January 1987

Hidin' From Love
Win Some, Lose Some
Wait And See
Give Me Your Love
Wastin' Time
Don't You Say It
Remember
State Of Mind
Try To See It My Way

YOU WANT IT, YOU GOT IT
(A & M Records)
producer Bob Clearmountain
UK release date April 1982
(UK#78, 24/8/85)

Lonely Nights
One Good Reason
Don't Look Now
Coming Home
Fits Ya Good
Jealousy
Tonight
You Want It, You Got It
Last Chance
No One Makes It Right

CUTS LIKE A KNIFE
(A & M Records)
producer Bob Clearmountain
UK release date March 1983
(US#8, 2/4/83; UK#30, 15/3/86; CAN#9, 22/2/83

The Only One
Take Me Back
This Time
Straight From The Heart
Cuts Like A Knife
I'm Ready
What's It Gonna Be
Don't Leave Me Lonely
The Best Was Yet To Come

RECKLESS
(A & M Records)
producer Bob Clearmountain
UK release date February 1985
(US#1, 1/12/84; UK#7, 2/3/85; CAN#1, 19/11/84)

One Night Love Affair
She's Only Happy When She's Dancing
Run To You
Heaven
Somebody
Summer Of '69
Kids Wanna Rock
Its Only Love
Long Gone
Ain't Gonna Cry

INTO THE FIRE
(A & M Records)
producer Bob Clearmountain
UK release date March 1987
(US#7, 19/4/87; UK#10, 11/4/87; CAN#1, 13/4/87)

Heat Of The Night
Into The Fire
Victim Of Love
Another Day
Native Son
Only The Strong Survive
Rebel
Remembrance Day
Hearts On Fire
Home Again

WAKING UP THE NEIGHBOURS
(A & M Records)
producer Robert 'Mutt' Lange
UK release date October 1991
(US#6, 12/10/91; UK#1, 12/10/91; CAN#1, 7/10/91)

Is Your Mama Gonna Miss Ya?
Hey Honey, I'm Packin' You In!
Can't Stop This Thing We Started
Thought I'd Died And Gone To Heaven
Not Guilty
Vanishing
House Arrest
Do I Have To Say The Words?
There Will Never Be Another Tonight
All I Want Is You
Depend On Me
(Everything I Do) I Do It For You
If You Wanna Leave Me (Can I Come Too?)
Touch The Hand
Don't Drop That Bomb On Me

SECTION 2: THE SINGLES

Hidin' From Love/Wait And See
(A & M Records; April 1980)

Lonely Nights/Don't Look Now
(A & M Records; November 1981)

Straight From The Heart/Fits Ya Good
(A & M Records; March 1983)
(US#10, 16/4/83; CAN#10, 30/5/83)

Cuts Like A Knife/Fits Ya Good
(A & M Records; September 1983)
(US#15, 25/6/83; CAN#9, 28/2/83)

One Good Reason
(A & M Records; January 1984)

Run To You/I'm Ready/Cuts Like A Knife
(A & M Records; December 1984)
(US#6, 24/11/84; UK#11, 12/1/85)

Somebody/Long Gone
(A & M Records; March 1985)
(US#11, 23/2/85; UK#35, 16/3/85; CAN#13, 25/2/85)

Heaven/Diana
(A & M Records; May 1985)
(US#1, 27/4/85; UK#38, 25/5/85; CAN#6, 3/6/85)

Summer Of '69/Kids Wanna Rock
(A & M Records; July 1985)
(US#5, 13/7/85; UK#42, 10/8/85; CAN#12, 22/7/85)

One Night Love Affair
(CAN#49, 4/11/85)

Its Only Love/The Best Is Yet To Come, with TINA TURNER
(A & M Records; November 1985)
(US#15, 7/12/85; UK#29, 2/11/85; CAN#12, 2/12/85)

Christmas Time/Reggae Christmas
(A & M Records; December 1985)
(UK#55, 21/12/85; CAN#39, 23/12/85)

This Time/I'm Ready
(A & M Records; February 1986)
(US#24, 1/10/83; UK#41, 22/2/86; CAN#28, 26/11/84)
(12" features Lonely Nights)

Straight From The Heart/Fits Ya Good
(A & M Records; June 1986)
(UK#51, 12/7/86)
(12" features a live version of Straight From
The Heart)
(Double pack includes Run Too Close / Somebody
/ One Good Reason)

Heat Of The Night/Another Day
(A & M Records; March 1987)
(US#6, 29/3/87; UK#50, 28/3/87; CAN#4, 6/5/87)

Hearts On Fire/Run To You
(A & M Records; May 1987)
(US#26, 13/6/87; UK#57, 20/6/87; CAN#37, 29/6/87)
(12" features Native Son)

Victim Of Love/Heat Of The Night - Live
(A & M Records; October 1987)
(US#32, 22/8/87; UK#68, 17/10/87)

**(Everything I Do) I Do It For You/
Reckless - Live/She's Only Happy When
She's Dancing**
(A & M Records; June 1991)
(US#1, 13/7/91; UK#1, 29/6/91; CAN#1, 8/7/91)
(12" features an extended version of
(Everything I Do) I Do It For You and
Cuts Like A Knife - Live)

**Can't Stop This Thing We Started
/Its Only Love - Live**
(A & M Records; September 1991)
(US#5, 28/9/91; UK#12, 14/9/91;
CAN#2, 23/9/91)

SECTION 3: THE VIDEO

RECKLESS - THE VIDEO
(A & M)

Run To You
Heaven
Somebody
Summer Of '69
Kids Wanna Rock
This Time